W9-COA-944

Montana

EXPLORE THE UNITED STATES

Julie Murray

Big Buddy BOOKS

Explore the United States

VISIT US AT
www.abdopublishing.com

Published by ABDO Publishing Company, PO Box 398166, Minneapolis, MN 55439.

Copyright © 2013 by Abdo Consulting Group, Inc. International copyrights reserved in all countries. No part of this book may be reproduced in any form without written permission from the publisher. Big Buddy Books™ is a trademark and logo of ABDO Publishing Company.

Printed in the United States of America, North Mankato, Minnesota.
042012
092012

 PRINTED ON RECYCLED PAPER

Coordinating Series Editor: Rochelle Baltzer
Editor: Sarah Tieck
Contributing Editors: Megan M. Gunderson, BreAnn Rumsch, Marcia Zappa
Graphic Design: Adam Craven
Cover Photograph: *Shutterstock*: mlorenz.
Interior Photographs/Illustrations: *Alamy*: Richard Cummins (p. 26), Everett Collection Inc (p. 25); *AP Photo*: AP Photo (p. 23), North Wind Picture Archives via AP Images (p. 13), Chris O'Meara, File (p. 23); *Getty Images*: Donald M. Jones/Minden Pictures (p. 17); *Glow Images*: Rob Crandall (p. 13), Diez, O. (p. 30); *iStockphoto*: ©iStockphoto.com/Aspheric (p. 29), ©iStockphoto.com/PhilAugustavo (p. 19), ©iStockphoto.com/outtakes (p. 30), ©iStockphoto.com/GeorgePeters (p. 27), ©iStockphoto.com/RiverNorthPhotography (p. 26), ©iStockphoto.com/RoseMaryBush (p. 30), ©iStockphoto.com/sdbower (p. 21), ©iStockphoto.com/step2626 (p. 11), ©iStockphoto.com/KeithSzafranski (p. 19), ©iStockphoto.com/wellesenterprises (p. 9); *Shutterstock*: Philip Lange (p. 30), Mike Norton (p. 5), Jim Parkin (p. 27), Sally Scott (p. 27), Katherine Welles (p. 9).

All population figures taken from the 2010 US census.

Library of Congress Cataloging-in-Publication Data

Murray, Julie, 1969-
  Montana / Julie Murray.
     p. cm. -- (Explore the United States)
  ISBN 978-1-61783-364-9
  1. Montana--Juvenile literature. I. Title.
  F731.3.M873 2012
  978.6--dc23
                        2012007219

MONTANA

Contents

ONE NATION

The United States is a **diverse** country. It has farmland, cities, coasts, and mountains. Its people come from many different backgrounds. And, its history covers more than 200 years.

Today the country includes 50 states. Montana is one of these states. Let's learn more about Montana and its story!

Did You Know?

Montana became a state on November 8, 1889. It was the forty-first state to join the nation.

4

Montana is known for its mountains. The Rocky Mountains cover part of the state.

5

MONTANA UP CLOSE

The United States has four main **regions**. Montana is in the West.

Montana has four states on its borders. North Dakota and South Dakota are east. Wyoming is south. Idaho is west. The country of Canada is north.

Montana is the fourth-largest state. Its total area is 147,039 square miles (380,829 sq km). About 1 million people live in this state.

REGIONS OF THE UNITED STATES

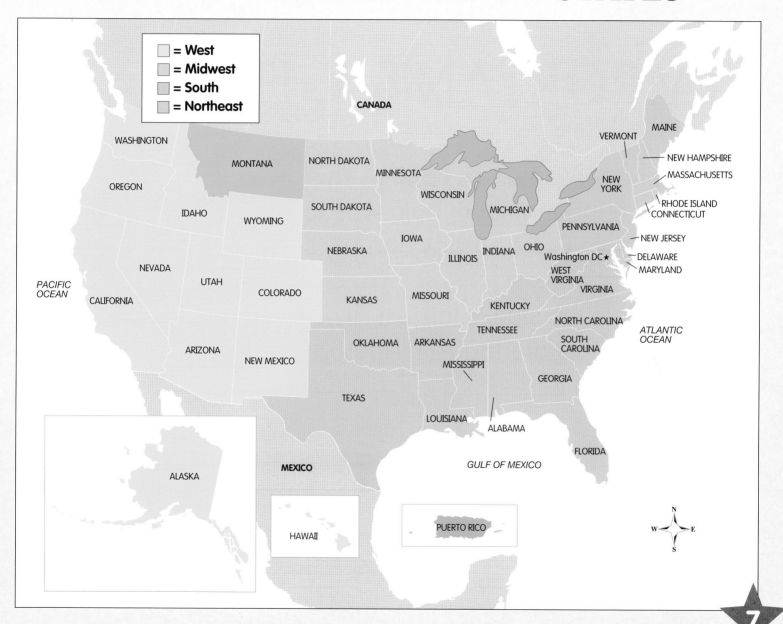

= West
= Midwest
= South
= Northeast

CANADA

WASHINGTON
MONTANA
NORTH DAKOTA
MINNESOTA
OREGON
IDAHO
WYOMING
SOUTH DAKOTA
WISCONSIN
MICHIGAN
IOWA
NEBRASKA
NEVADA
UTAH
COLORADO
KANSAS
MISSOURI
ILLINOIS
INDIANA
OHIO
CALIFORNIA
ARIZONA
NEW MEXICO
OKLAHOMA
ARKANSAS
KENTUCKY
TENNESSEE
TEXAS
LOUISIANA
MISSISSIPPI
ALABAMA
GEORGIA
NORTH CAROLINA
SOUTH CAROLINA
VIRGINIA
WEST VIRGINIA
Washington DC ★
PENNSYLVANIA
NEW YORK
VERMONT
MAINE
NEW HAMPSHIRE
MASSACHUSETTS
RHODE ISLAND
CONNECTICUT
NEW JERSEY
DELAWARE
MARYLAND
FLORIDA

PACIFIC OCEAN
ATLANTIC OCEAN
GULF OF MEXICO

ALASKA
MEXICO
HAWAII
PUERTO RICO

N
W E
S

IMPORTANT CITIES

Helena is Montana's **capital**. This city was founded in 1864. Around that time, gold was found in a creek called Last Chance Gulch. Today, the city's Main Street is in this area.

Billings is the state's largest city. It is home to 104,170 people. In the late 1800s, Billings grew as railroads were built through it.

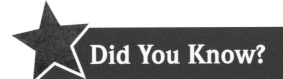

Did You Know?

Billings was named for Frederick Billings. He was the president of the Northern Pacific Railway Company.

★★
The Montana State Capitol opened in 1902.

Montana

●Great Falls

●Missoula
★Helena

●Billings

N
W E
S

★★★★★★★★★★★★★★★★★★★★★★★★★★★★
Billings has important businesses,
such as companies that make food.

9

Missoula is Montana's second-largest city. It has 66,788 people. Firefighters train there to fight forest fires. Also, the University of Montana is in this city.

Great Falls is the state's third-largest city. It is home to 58,505 people. The Great Falls of the Missouri River are there. They provide power.

Black Eagle Dam is one of several dams on the Missouri River near Great Falls.

Montana in History

Montana's history includes Native Americans, explorers, and settlers. Native Americans have lived in present-day Montana for thousands of years.

In 1803, President Thomas Jefferson bought land in the **Louisiana Purchase**. This included most of what is now Montana. Soon, people moved to the area to look for gold, mine, and farm. Montana became a US territory in 1864 and a state in 1889.

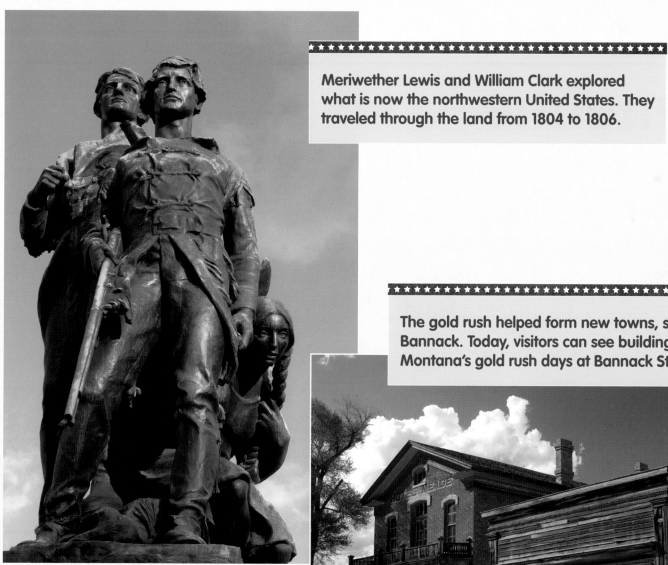

Meriwether Lewis and William Clark explored what is now the northwestern United States. They traveled through the land from 1804 to 1806.

The gold rush helped form new towns, such as Bannack. Today, visitors can see buildings from Montana's gold rush days at Bannack State Park.

Timeline

1876

About 260 US soldiers and 2,000 Native Americans fought at the Battle of the Little Bighorn. This occurred after many years of fighting over land.

1862

A gold rush started in Montana.

1800s

William Clark carved his name on a large rock near the Yellowstone River. He named it to honor a member of the Lewis and Clark Expedition. It became known as Pompey's Pillar.

The Northern Pacific Railway Company built the first railroad through Billings.

Montana became the forty-first state on November 8.

1882 1889

1806

1916

Jeannette Rankin of Missoula became the first woman elected to the US House of Representatives. She served in Congress from 1917 to 1919 and from 1941 to 1943.

2011

Walter Bruening of Great Falls died on April 14. At 114 years old, he was the world's oldest living man!

1900s

2000s

Oil was found in eastern Montana. Soon, many wells were built in the area to pump oil from the ground.

Wildfires burned more than 500,000 acres (200,000 ha) of land in western Montana.

Pompey's Pillar became a national monument.

2000

2001

1951

15

ACROSS THE LAND

Montana has **plains**, forests, and mountains. The Rocky Mountains run through western Montana. Major rivers include the Missouri and the Yellowstone. **Glacier** National Park and part of Yellowstone National Park are in this state, too.

Many types of animals make their homes in Montana. These include grizzly bears, bison, prairie dogs, and eagles.

Did You Know?

In July, the average temperature in Montana is 68°F (20°C). In January, it is 18°F (-8°C).

Special areas have been set aside in Montana to protect animals such as bison.

Earning a Living

Montana has important businesses. Many people work in service jobs, such as helping visitors to the state.

Montana also has important natural **resources**. Coal and oil are removed from deep under the **plains**. Farmers in Montana grow wheat, barley, and hay.

★★★★★★★★★★★★★★★★★★★★★
Montana has important gold, copper, and lead mines.

★★★★★★★★★★★★★★★★★★★★★
Montana farmers raise livestock, including sheep and beef cattle.

19

Natural Wonder

Glacier National Park is in northwestern Montana. It is named for the glaciers that once covered the land. Over time, they melted and shaped the land into beautiful mountains and valleys.

In 1910, more than 1 million acres (400,000 ha) of land was set aside for the park. It has lakes, mountains, and forests.

Did You Know?

About 25 glaciers are found in Glacier National Park today.

Glacier National Park is one of the most visited places in Montana. People camp, hike, and canoe there.

21

Hometown Heroes

Many famous people have lived in Montana. Evel Knievel was born in Butte (BYOOT) in 1938. His given name was Robert Knievel. He was a famous motorcycle rider.

People called Knievel a daredevil for his daring motorcycle **stunts**. He did more than 300 jumps. One time, he jumped over 13 buses on his motorcycle! Another time, he jumped over a tank of sharks!

Large crowds came to see Knievel's stunts.

Knievel was known for wearing red, white, and blue suits. His motorcycles were often decorated this way, too.

23

Calamity Jane was born in Missouri in 1852 as Martha Jane Cannary. She moved to Montana with her family in 1865.

Calamity Jane became known for riding horses and shooting guns. She showed off these skills in Wild West shows. These shows featured plays, cowboys, and wild animals.

Calamity Jane wore men's clothing, which was unusual for women at that time.

Tour Book

Do you want to go to Montana? If you visit the state, here are some places to go and things to do!

 ## Discover

Spend time at Pictograph Cave State Park near Billings. One of the caves has rock paintings called pictographs. Native Americans made these thousands of years ago.

 ## Remember

Visit the Little Bighorn Battlefield National Monument. It honors soldiers and Native Americans who fought in the Battle of the Little Bighorn. Hundreds of people died in the battle.

 Ride

Explore Beartooth Highway. This is a famous mountain road. It is surrounded by three national forests. At 10,350 feet (3,155 m), it is the highest road in Montana!

Race

Hit the slopes! Skiing and other outdoor sports are popular in Montana.

Explore

Go for a hike in Yellowstone National Park. It is the oldest national park in the world!

A Great State

The story of Montana is important to the United States. The people and places that make up this state offer something special to the country. Together with all the states, Montana helps make the United States great.

Avalanche Lake is one of Montana's natural wonders. Each spring, melting snow slides down the surrounding mountain slopes in avalanches and waterfalls.

Fast Facts

Date of Statehood:
November 8, 1889

Population (rank):
989,415
(44th most-populated state)

Total Area (rank):
147,039 square miles
(4th largest state)

Motto:
"Oro y Plata"
(Gold and Silver)

Nickname:
Treasure State,
Big Sky Country

State Capital:
Helena

Flag:

Flower: Bitterroot

Postal Abbreviation:
MT

Tree: Ponderosa Pine

Bird: Western Meadowlark

Important Words

capital a city where government leaders meet.

diverse made up of things that are different from each other.

glacier (GLAY-shuhr) a huge chunk of ice and snow on land.

Louisiana Purchase land the United States purchased from France in 1803. It extended from the Mississippi River to the Rocky Mountains and from Canada through the Gulf of Mexico.

plains flat or rolling land without trees.

region a large part of a country that is different from other parts.

resource a supply of something useful or valued.

stunt an action requiring great skill or daring.

Web Sites

To learn more about Montana, visit ABDO Publishing Company online. Web sites about Montana are featured on our Book Links page. These links are routinely monitored and updated to provide the most current information available.

www.abdopublishing.com

Index